A Week in the Blue Mountains

DISTANT VIEW OF SHARTLESVILLE

A Week in the Blue Mountains

The Record of a Happy Outing

Henry W. Shoemaker

(Author of *Pennsylvania Mountain Stories*)

an imprint of Sunbury Press, Inc.
Mechanicsburg, PA USA

an imprint of Sunbury Press, Inc.
Mechanicsburg, PA USA

FIRST DISTELFINK PRESS EDITION: February 2026

Set in Adobe Garamond | Interior design by Crystal Devine | Cover by Lawrence Knorr | Edited by Lawrence Knorr.

Publisher's Cataloging-in-Publication Data
Names: Shoemaker, Henry W., author; Knorr, Lawrence K., foreword.
Title: A week in the blue mountains : the record of a happyy outing / Henry W. Shoemaker.
Description: First trade paperback edition. | Mechanicsburg, PA : Distelfink Press, 2026.
Summary: Henry Wharton Shoemaker, the newspaperman and author, traveled the edge of the Blue Mountain in the Summer of 1914 with his wife, Mabelle Ruth Ord Shoemaker, noting the hotels at which they stayed, the people met, and the sites seen..
Identifiers: ISBN : 979-8-88819-448-5 (paperback).
Subjects: TRAVEL / United States / Northeast / Middle Atlantic | BIOGRAPHY & AUTOBIOGRAPHY / Memoirs | HISTORY / United States / State & Local / Middle Atlantic.

Designed in the USA
0 1 1 2 3 5 8 13 21 34 55

For the Love of Books!

Cover art is a portion of the painting *Path in the White Mountains* by Christopher High Shearer, 1876.

To Mrs. H. W. S.

THE AGREEABLE COMPANION OF THE OUTING.
THESE PAGES ARE SINCERELY DEDICATED.

"Men who undertake only one district are much more likely to advance natural knowledge than those who grasp at more than they can possibly be acquainted with; every kingdom, every province, should have its Own Monographer." —Rev. Gilbert White

CONTENTS

THE DELECTABLE MOUNTAINS

Foreword

FROM June 14 to June 22, 1914, Henry Wharton Shoemaker and his wife, Mabelle Ruth Ord Shoemaker, traversed the Blue Mountain by carriage and on horseback, starting in Reading, Pennsylvania, in Berks County, and then weaving through northern Berks to western Lehigh, then Schuylkill, Dauphin, and Lebanon Counties, before returning to Reading. The couple had been married the prior year, and they appeared to enjoy each other's company. Along the way, they had picnics together, and Mabelle took photographs, some of which are shared in this book.

Always the storyteller, Henry enhanced the travel details with vignettes about the locals he met or about those who had lived in the locations in the past. The vast majority of Shoemaker's recounting appears to be true, with a few exceptions, all noted in the footnotes. Perhaps Henry was on his best behavior.

One of the stranger moments was when, nearing Virginville, Berks County, he suggested the name is a variation of the French name Vergennesville, implying the former French diplomat, Charles Gravier, comte de Vergennes, had something to do with the former Native American site. Of course, the name is rather in alignment with the nearby Maiden Creek, harkening back to a Native American legend. One can imagine this well-to-do couple picnicking by a stream with their noses turned up, discussing the merits of French diplomacy during the American Revolution and then attaching it to the locale.

At the time of this adventure, Henry had just published *Stories of Great Pennsylvania Hunters* (1913) and *In the Seven Mountains* (1913) and was releasing *Black Forest Souvenirs* (1914), *Pennsylvania Lion or Panther* (1914), and *Wolf Days in Pennsylvania* (1914). A common thread through the earlier works was stories about panthers, lynxes, and bobcats. During the travel memoir, Henry recounts several big cat hunters from the area.

Of course, Henry was well-connected and met with various leaders and proprietors along the way, including a descendant of Conrad Weiser and Henry Melchior Muhlenberg. He also connected with the painter Christopher High Shearer, known for his landscapes.

What results is a unique time capsule of the people and places on both sides of the first mountain in the heart of Pennsylvania Dutch country. For this edition, the journal has been broken out by day and time, according to the original itinerary. Additional photographs have been added to further illustrate what or whom they saw. All the photographs have been carefully restored, sharpened, and colorized to provide a fresh look with details often lost in old black and white images.

Lawrence Knorr, Ph.D.
February 2026

Introduction

THIS is a record of an eight-day drive through one of the most picturesque and historic sections of Pennsylvania. It is written as a plea to "see Pennsylvania first." While the United States and foreign lands abound with interesting and romantic spots, right at our very doors, in the Keystone State, we have enough that is well worth seeing to keep travelers busily engaged for a lifetime. After one has become acquainted with his or her native state, it is time to travel to other states or other lands. Traveling through inland Pennsylvania is attractive in many ways. The roads are, for the most part, splendid at least for horses and carriages, and anyone wishing to admire scenery or study local history and traditions or to make checklists of birds and wild flowers can find satisfaction in no other way. The hotels in the region visited in this Blue Mountain trip were above the average of excellence. The beds were good, everything was clean, and the fare was simple but good. The landlords were invariably polite, and this feature was put to a real test, as in almost every instance our party arrived at the inns an hour or two after the regular supper hour. We cooked our mid-day meals in the woods, being provided with a small outfit, which consisted principally of a "roaster," a gridiron-like appliance on four legs, obtained from D. T. Abercrombie,[1] New York, and useful in many ways, a coffee pot, a frying pan, some cheap knives and forks, wooden dishes, and some George Washington,[2] or instantaneous coffee. While we were armed with a permit to camp on the state lands, we probably did most of the cooking on private property.

1. David Thomas Abercrombie (June 6, 1867 – August 29, 1931) was the founder of the American brand Abercrombie & Fitch. A topographer and expert in the outdoors, Abercrombie opened the company as New York's outfitter for the elite and later partnered up with co-founder Ezra Fitch – both men managed the Company through great years of success. (Wikipedia)

2. Not our George Washington of Revolutionary War fame! George Constant Louis Washington (May 20, 1871 – March 29, 1946) was a Belgian-British inventor and businessman. He is best remembered for his improvement of an early instant coffee process and for the company he founded to mass-produce it, the G. Washington Coffee Company. (Wikipedia)

We used every precaution to extinguish the fires before leaving, and gathered up all papers and rubbish, so as to leave the grounds as neat as we found them. The prevalence of springs of clear, pure water all through these mountains made camping a most delightful experience. The prices at the hotels where we stopped for the nights were very reasonable, the general charge being four dollars for supper, breakfast and lodging for two persons and driver and two meals each for a pair of horses. We hired our team in Reading, where there are several good liveries. In order to fully enjoy the Blue Mountain country, a driver speaking Pennsylvania German is essential. This is a passport to the confidence and goodwill of the people, especially the older ones, who, when gained, are ready and anxious to answer questions of all kinds. The Pennsylvania "Dutchman" is shy by nature and inclined to be suspicious of strangers when living in remote localities, but a word or two in his favorite tongue soon puts him at his ease, and he has a heart of gold. It is recommended that for reference, the following books be taken on a drive into the Blue Ridge: D. C. Henning's *Tales of the Blue Mountains*, Chester A. Reed's *Land Birds of America*, Mrs. William Starr Dana's *How to Know the Wild Flowers*, *Getting Acquainted with the Trees* by Horace McFarland, and a pocket map of Pennsylvania. We usually drove thirty miles a day, but on some occasions covered forty without any difficulty. It is hoped that others will enjoy this particularly charming drive.

Henry W. Shoemaker,
Fairbrook, Pennsylvania, June 26, 1914.

A WEEK IN THE BLUE MOUNTAINS

(The Record of a Happy Outing.)

Arrived Reading, Pa.

Stopped at American House: excellent hotel; modern in every way.

June 14, 1914, 5:55 P.M.

IT was late in the afternoon of June fourteenth when the train neared Reading. We were reminded of the immortal Bayard Taylor's[3] description of his approach to that city:

> We presently emerged upon a slope, whence a glorious landscape opened upon my eyes. Never had I seen or imagined anything so beautiful. The stately old town lay below, stretched at full length on an inclined plane, rising from the Schuylkill to the base of the mountain; the river, winding in abrupt curves, disclosed itself here and there through the landscape; hills of superb undulation rose and fell, in interlinking lines, through the middle distance, Scull's Hill boldly detaching itself in front, and far in the north the Blue Ridge lifted its dim wall against the sky. The sinking sun turned the smokes of the town and the vapors of the river to golden dust, athwart of which gleamed the coloring of the distant woods. The noises of the scene were softened and mellowed, and above them all, sweet and faint, sounded the bugle of a boatman on the canal. It was not ignorant admiration on my part, for one familiar with the grandest aspects of Nature must still confess that few towns on this side of the Atlantic are so nobly environed.

And these words, written many years ago, portray the Reading of today, the nascent Paris of America. When we reached the main or "outer"

3. Bayard Taylor (January 11, 1825 – December 19, 1878) was an American poet, literary critic, translator, travel author, and diplomat. As a poet, he was very popular, with a crowd of more than 4,000 attending a poetry reading once, which was a record that stood for 85 years. His travelogues were popular in both the United States and Great Britain. He served in diplomatic posts in Russia and Prussia. (Wikipedia)

station of the Reading Railway,[4] great crowds of happy travelers were assembled. We pushed our way through the throngs to the cab-stand, presided over by the genial Billy Rogers.[5] We were soon in a comfortable coupe, drawn by a plodding horse and being driven along the shady, sunset streets to the American House,[6] at the foot of the majestic Penn Square. There we found more friendly faces to greet us, the proprietors, clerks, and bellboys vying with one another to make us comfortable. After supper, in the cool of the evening, we rode out to the foot of Mount Penn and boarded the gravity car for a ride through the sweet-scented woods.[7] It was so cool and primeval in that forest-hidden route that we scarcely realized that almost below us, quarrymen were blasting away the verdant face of the mountain. Posterity will blame our heedless generation for this! On the return trip, the car was filled with merry-makers, who laughed and joked until it came to a halt at the station. It was a gay, care-free scene, one not likely to be forgotten.

---

4. The "Reading Railroad" of Monopoly fame, officially named the Philadelphia and Reading Railway.

5. There are two William Rogers buried in Charles Evans Cemetery in Reading. William H. Rogers (August 5, 1861 – April 28, 1923) would have been 53 years old at the time of these events. William Shaffer Rogers (May 22, 1872 – February 16, 1953) would have been 42.

6. The American House was located at the corner of 4th and Penn Streets (354 Penn Street) in Reading. It began as Housum's Hotel in the mid-1850s, evolving into a grand hotel with a cupola and iron balcony, becoming a prominent spot with a famous restaurant and lodging, including a 1910 addition.

7. From Corrie Crupi's article "The Gravity Railroad" at the Berks History Center (https://berkshistory.org/article/the-gravity-railroad/): "Inspired by the Mauch Chunk Switchback, there is no grander view anywhere. A glorious panoramic 30-mile view and a changing kaleidoscope of beauty connected the mountains, the city, and the river. The Gravity Railroad provided the excitement of a mountain ascent through the beautiful glen overlooking Mineral Spring Park and onward into Egleman's Park through the heart of the cool and shaded forest where the air is pure, and the water is clean, and across Skyline Drive to the "Summit" at the top of the Mountain. Convinced that the Gravity Line needed something at the summit for attraction, the company, in 1890, built a magnificent stone dance pavilion known as the Tower Hotel."

PENN SQUARE AT NIGHT, CIRCA 1915

Left Reading

Drove out of town through Mineral Springs Park. Stopped at Zoo.

June 15, 7:30 A.M.

THE next morning, not much after seven o'clock, the surrey team and driver that were to convey us to the delectable mountains drew up to the door of the hotel. Lemon Killian,[8] our guide on many previous trips, was driver, and we were glad to see his smiling face once more. We started away promptly, through the sunlit, bright, clean, streets in the direction of the Kutztown Pike.[9] It was dusty from many motor cars, but we could enjoy the sight of many snug farms, well-kept and beautifully shaded, along the way. The cherries were ripening, and the delicious odor of catalpa blossoms was in the air.

8. A Lemon Wesley Killian (September 12, 1876 – August 8, 1931) is buried at Saint John's United Church of Christ Cemetery in Gibraltar, Berks County, Pennsylvania.

9. Today, this is the Kutztown Road. From the American House, the party likely traveled north on 4th Street to Greenwich, and then north on 9th Street, where it merges into Kutztown Road.

Arrived Kirbyville

Quaint old inn; fine scenery.

Noon

WE stopped for dinner at the quaint old halfway[10] house at Kirbyville.[11] It was a stone structure with thick walls and low ceilings, probably a century old. In front grew a line of huge linden trees, making the effect of a bower.

After dinner, we sat on the porch, as a shower arose, which laid the dust and sent travelers a-horse or on foot, hurrying to join us in our place of shelter. After the rain, the birds began singing again. There were many different kinds. Robins predominated, but there were flickers, orioles, brown thrushes, black birds, and song sparrows. Then and there we resolved to make a list of the rarer birds we would meet with on our drive.

Far oft on the Penn's Mount range we could hear a woodchopper's regular click, click, click. It must have been three miles away, but the sounds came to us distinctly through the stillness. As we climbed into our surrey, a bobwhite's melodious call was audible in the waving wheat field across the way.

10. Meaning an establishment between two towns.

11. The Kirbyville Inn is now an antique store. Originally known as the White Horse Tavern, it was built circa 1790.

KIRBYVILLE

Arrived Kutztown

Visited Keystone State Normal School. Good roads.

2:30 P.M.

THE sun was shining brightly when we drove into the shady street of old Kutztown, home of history and high thinking. We stopped before the main building of the Keystone State Normal School[12] and inquired of a smiling, fair-haired girl if Professor Deatrick[13] was on the premises. She ran into the building, coming out a moment later with the happy intelligence that he would excuse his class in five minutes and be with us. It was a short five minutes, and then the kindly-faced educator joined us, taking us for a tour of the buildings of this model institution. All was bright and airy, and a savoring of modern methods. We met Professor Grim,[14] who discovered the parasite of the San Jose scale, and President Rothermel,[15] one of this country's leading younger educators.

After inspecting the unfinished library, which will be a gem of its kind, we were prepared for another treat, a visit to Mr. Henry K. Deisher's

12. The original Old Main at what is now Kutztown University was built in 1866 and destroyed by fire in 1924.

13. Rev. Dr. William Wilberforce Deatrick, A.M., Sc.D. (1853 – 1925), taught English, Psychology, Pedagogy, and Photography at Keystone State Normal School from 1891 until 1923. Today's Deatrick Hall is named in his honor. He is buried at Fairview Cemetery in Kutztown.

14. Professor James Stewart Grim (October 21, 1873 – May 18, 1949), an 1893 graduate of Kutztown State Normal School, was a beloved and long-serving science and agriculture instructor at KSNS (now Kutztown University), teaching for over 45 years and influencing generations, with the Grim Science Building later named in his honor. He is buried at Fairview Cemetery in Kutztown.

15. Dr. Amos C. Rothermel (January 6, 1864 – October 5, 1946) served as the Principal of Kutztown State Normal School (1901-1928) and then the first President of Kutztown State Teachers College (1928-1934). He is buried at Hope Cemetery in Kutztown.

collection of Indian relics.[16] We found Mr. Deisher a charming, polished man, interested in many things; versatility seems to be his watchword, as he is a manufacturer, banker, farmer, gardener, florist, historian, archaeologist and antiquarian. First of all, he took us through his ginseng garden, where he raises this root, which is so precious to the Chinese. It grows under a covering of laths, placed a couple of inches apart, so as to resemble the forest shade. Mr. Deisher also raises Golden Seal, Senega Root, Pink Root and other medicinal plants in smaller quantities. He is also making a specialty of raising wild flowers of species in danger of extinction through the destruction of their natural forest covers. But the Indian collection is worth a day's visit alone. It comprises the arrows, spears, and implements of Pennsylvania Indians, as well as pottery. The gem of the collection is a Pennsylvania Indian pot, the most perfect example in existence as far as is known. The collection of California Indian baskets, from huge ones down to some little bigger than a shoe button, is said to be the finest in the world. As many of the tribes that made these baskets are dying out, they can never be duplicated in the future. There is also a collection of articles belonging to the early Pennsylvania Germans, such as lanterns, cowbells, spoons, dishes, mirrors, chairs, tables, sausage-makers, candle molds, rare prints, and so on. But we had to hurry away; we had promised friends that we would meet them at Crystal Cave[17] at six-thirty.

---

16. Henry K. Deisher (March 12, 1867 – November 4, 1951) was a partner and later sole owner of the Deisher Knitting Mills, Kutztown. He served as an assistant curator at the State Museum in Harrisburg from 1928 until he retired in 1940. Widely known for his collection of Indian relics and antiques, he was recognized as an authority on Pennsylvania Indian lore. A collection bearing his name is in the State Museum. Deisher was one of the collectors who interacted with D. B. Brunner, the author of *The Indians of Berks County, Pennsylvania.*

17. Crystal Cave is west of Kutztown, on the way to Virginville.

REV. PROF. WILLIAM WILBERFORCE DEATRICK, A.M., SC.D.

HENRY K. DEISHER

FACULTY IN FRONT OF THE KUTZTOWN NORMAL SCHOOL

SPECIMEN OF PENNSLVANIA INDIAN POTTERY
(In Collection of H. K. Deisher, Kutztown, Pa.)

Arrived Crystal Cave

Crystal Cave Hotel, well kept.

6:30 P.M.

THROUGH the delightful mellowness of the golden hour, we were driven from the town. We paused once on a hill and looked back on the town, lying there so peacefully on the ridge, the buildings barely appearing above the buttresses of noble trees. Beyond were fertile fields and green hills. Surely a most inspiring spot to live in or obtain an education. To Crystal Cave, the road wound in and out among the hills, beneath a continuous canopy of trees. The quail were whistling in the meadows, the robins were caroling their even-songs, rabbits eyed us curiously from the middle of the road before hopping away into tall grass. It was a drive of sheer delight!

At last we came to a crossroads where a fingerboard pointed: "To Crystal Cave, ¼ m." The road which we followed led through a narrow gorge, with steep, wheat-covered hills on either side, and a gurgling brook running through beds of calamus at the roadside.[18] We caught sight of the strange old hotel,[19] the home of ghosts and strange, sinister episodes, hidden behind the spreading Norway maple trees. Artist Shearer,[20] who was to meet us there, came forward, with his great white beard blown by the evening breeze, looking more like Leonardo da Vinci's self-portrait in the Uffizi Gallery than ever! Landlord Kohler[21] joined him, and we were given a genial welcome.

---

18. Today this is called Crystal Cave Road.

19. Known as the Kohler Hotel or Cave House.

20. Christopher High Shearer (1846-1926) was a prominent Berks County, Pennsylvania landscape artist, known for his detailed nature scenes, influential role in founding the Reading Public Museum (serving as its first art curator), and for teaching many local artists.

21. Samuel D. F. Kohler (1840-1908) discovered Crystal Cave in 1871 and became its first operator, with his family running the show cave and its associated hotel for generations. Son David A. Kohler (1865-1949) was the proprietor when the Shoemakers visited.

The weird old place looked unchanged, as we climbed the narrow stairs to our room, which had windows on two sides, and was furnished in the style of fifty years ago—even to the marble-topped table. About a dozen of us sat down to a supper of chicken and waffles, which we enjoyed, while the good-natured landlord apologized because the fish in the Saconey did not bite that afternoon—else it would have been a fish supper, he said.

After the repast, we visited the cave, which, alas, had lost some of its mystery since electric lights were installed.[22] Even the bats had deserted it, we learned. Perhaps they had gone across the hill to the pristine glooms of the Dragon's Cave at Dreibelbis![23]

The stars were out when we left the cavern, and we walked in single file, led by the landlord with one of his old-time copper lanterns, along the avenue of ghost-like junipers. We decided to visit the ghost room in the attic of the hotel before going to bed; it would give us an eerie feeling for retiring! Still led by Mr. Kohler and his copper lantern, we climbed to the floor under the roof. The door to the little room beneath the eaves was open, just as it was when a belated traveler who awoke at midnight to find the rival to his wife's affections standing by the bedside, and, after giving the fancied being a kick, which went through space and through the plastered partition, fled precipitously downstairs. We made a weird appearance, grouped about in the flickering, yellow light, in the moldy, stuffy little room.

On the way downstairs, we took a look at the secret room, which is between the newer and older parts of the house. There may be a ghost in that room!

Before going to bed, we sat outside, in the growing gale, while the landlord told of the mysterious deaths of two of his hired men. One was found standing on his head, dead, behind the counter in the restaurant in the cellar, while the other, after spending a winter at the county home, twenty-three miles away, became homesick and tramped back, one night, dying from exhaustion in the haymow, where he had dragged himself for a nap before daylight.

22. At the time (1914), the cave utilized a Delco battery pack lighting system. When the cave was first opened to the public in 1872, visitors used torches and candles for light.

23. Less than a mile west, near Virginville.

When we reached our room, the gale was blowing furiously. We left the windows open and could hear it pounding against the ghostly old house off and on all night. The giant trees swayed and tossed, and some of them creaked and groaned.

In the morning, which was very clear and comparatively calm, we found many crisp maple twigs strewn about the road and lawns. We were out at six o'clock and climbed to the top of a high knoll by the hotel, where we obtained a superb view of the Blue Mountains. The storm had removed every vestige of humidity, and the landscape was as distinct, and the sky was as blue as a day in October. The atmosphere was positively cold.

CRYSTAL CAVE HOTEL

CHRISTOPHER HIGH SHEARER

Left Crystal Cave

Dinner at Lynnport, site of Fort Everett.

June 16, 6:30 A.M.

AFTER breakfast, we said *au revoir* to our good friends and started on our way. We left the little gorge, where the wind was winnowing the grain, and were soon driving along the banks of the sparkling Saconey.

At Virginville, or more properly Vergennesville,[24] the Saconey merges its destiny with the Ontelaunee or "sister" brook and flows away as Maiden Creek. We followed the Ontelaunee as far as Lenhartsville,[25] and it was a most entrancing drive. At first, the banks were lined with ancient white oaks, and we saw several green herons, which flew swiftly into the brushwood at our approach. Later on, hemlocks grew close to the banks, and the road was high above the stream, sometimes the precipice being nearly a hundred feet.

On his first drive along the Ontelaunee, in June 1911, the author composed the following:

OUT ALONG THE ONTELAUNEE.

In the sunshine sways the woodbine;
The evening primrose pouting;
The meadow-lark is singing,
The red-shouldered blackbird winging,
Out along the Ontelaunee.

Shafts of light like golden arrows,
Shooting through the white oak coverts;

---

24. There is no record of Virginville ever being associated with the Revolutionary War figure, the Frenchman Charles Gravier, Comte de Vergennes. Shoemaker might be overthinking this one.

25. This would be north along Dreibelbis Road.

The Halcyon is skimming,
A belated grebe is swimming,
Out along the Ontelaunee.

Antwerp blue the swelling current,
Grass-green are the banks that meet it,
O'er the rocks the water falling,
Sweeps around a turtle lolling.
Out along the Ontelaunee.

There's a sweetness in the breezes,
Blowing from the blooming clover;
The laurel on the hill;
The iris by the rill,
Out along the Ontelaunee.

The wild lupine and the blueweed;
On a path, a bright-eyed rabbit;
The pileated woodpecker provokes
Squirrels' chatter in the oaks.
Out along the Ontelaunee.

Through the vistas loom the mountains,
Spitzenberg and lofty Pinnacle,
Where the graceful buzzard soars.
And a wind mysterious roars.
Out along the Ontelaunee.

In the sunshine sways the woodbine,
The partridge vine is peeping.
The wood-robin's bell-like notes.
The bob-white calling in the oats,
Out along the Ontelaunee.

Stream of rare and radiant beauty,
Man's rude hands have marred it not;
Where the soul expands and blesses
Scenes where God His plan expresses,
Out along the Ontelaunee.

From Lenhartsville, we drove towards Lynnport, where we stopped for dinner.[26] This little village is of some renown as having been the site of Fort Everett,[27] built for defense against the Indians in 1756. We made the acquaintance of a very cultivated gentleman, Dr. D. A. Fulweiler,[28] who owns the site of the fort. He escorted us to the spot, which was in the center of a wheat field and on the outskirts of the village. He explained that he did not know that the structure had been the fort until 1885, when his workmen, in tearing it down, called his attention to the musketry loopholes. Shortly afterward, Edward Everett, the distinguished Massachusetts statesman, visited the village to see the fort which had been erected by one of his ancestors, and was much disappointed when he learned that it was no longer standing. Dr. Fulweiler told of the days when he was a boy, when wild pigeons were so plentiful. They flew northward in April to nest, but if they encountered heavy snowstorms, they would turn back. On one occasion, the ground at Lynnport was covered with snow, and the town boys amused themselves by throwing snowballs at the pigeons as they flew in vast companies over the hilltops.

From the site of the old fort, we continued our way to New Tripoli, which once boasted of a famous carriage works, but in these automobiling, tangoing days has been succeeded by a hosiery mill. The old Lutheran churchyard, where lie many Wanamakers, Kistlers, Mossers, Trexlers, and scions of other old families, is well worth a visit.

From thence we turned westward, towards the Blue Mountains, passing many fine highland farms. We stopped to inquire the way at the quaint old inn at Jacksonville and paused for a few minutes at the abandoned town called Slateville, once of high repute for its slate quarries.

---

26. Lynnport is about ten miles north of Lenhartsville, following the Kings Highway.

27. Fort Everett was a blockhouse, erected about 1756. It was a place of refuge and defense against raids in French and Indian War days. Troops here guarded the area just south of the Blue Mountain, between the Schuylkill and Lehigh Rivers.

28. Most likely, Shoemaker is referring to Dr. David W. Follweiler (1841-1924), who lived in the area and is buried at New Tripoli.

LENHARTSVILLE

Arrived Steinsville

Fine scenery and views of Blue Mountains.

6:30 P.M.

THE day had passed happily and quickly; it was in the golden hour again when we drew up before the old-fashioned inn at Steinsville.[29] Genial landlord Berk[30] was on hand to greet us and we were escorted into comfortable quarters. Back of the inn is a big yard, where sales of livestock were formerly held, but which now serves as a runway for the landlord's cows and chickens. The old barn possessed that cozy appearance so notable in George Moreland's[31] pictures.

After supper, we gazed at the golden light banking itself behind the Blue Mountains, being thankful to be in such a beautiful spot, and with the power to appreciate it to some extent. Down the village street, we heard quite a commotion and learned that a traveling show was giving a modified Wild West performance.[32] We met the showman, his wife and three little children, spending a half hour very pleasantly with them in their tent.

Then we walked down the street to the creamery and made our first purchase for our "gipsying,"[33] a pound of delicious butter. At this cream-

29. The Steinsville Hotel in Lehigh County was a historic inn in the village of Steinsville (now part of Kempton), serving travelers and locals at the crossroads of Steinsville Road and Blue Mountain House Road, evolving from its 19th-century roots as a community hub with a store and post office into a lodging facility.

30. Daniel P. Berk (September 13, 1858 – May 4, 1917) was the landlord of the Steinsville Hotel. He died of pneumonia, aged 58 years. He was a son of Daniel and Mary Berk, both deceased, and was a native of Albany Township, Berks County. He followed farming until 17 years ago, when he became proprietor of the Albany Hotel, later moving to the Steinsville Hotel.

31. The English landscape painter.

32. Most likely this was affiliated with the 101 Ranch Wild West Show, run by Joseph Carson Miller (1868-1927). The show came to Harrisburg and Allentown in early July 1914 and may have been passing through. If Shoemaker met Joe Miller, the wife was Lizzie and the children likely Alice (16), George (12), and Joe Jr. (8).

33. Picnicking.

ery, we were told that most of the output goes to a prominent dealer in Philadelphia.

Then we returned to the showman's tent and waited for the performance to begin. The roping and Wild West antics were excellent, well worth the paltry sum charged for admission.

STEINSVILLE HOTEL

JOSEPH CARSON MILLER

Left Steinsville

Beautiful drive to Eckville, with views of Pinnacle; magnificent drive across mountain to Windsor Furnace.

June 17, 6:30 A.M.

THE next morning dawned bright and clear; we were on the road early. The country towards "Allemaengel," which signified "All Wants," or everything provided, but foolishly changed to Albany, was rolling, with hay cutting in progress, girls and women working in the fields. Back of everything, from every bill, above every ravine, loomed the giant outlines of the Pinnacle, the highest peak of the Blue Ridge in Pennsylvania. It closely resembles Tahawns or Mt. Marcy in the Adirondacks. Around its summit, which seemed to have kinship to the blue dome, graceful buzzards, or "Berks County Eagles," as they are called, were soaring.

We purchased our camping outfit at Bailey's General Store, in Allemaengel and resumed our way towards Eckville.[34] In this upper point of Berks County occurs the famous "amphitheater" where the mountains form an almost complete circle, reminding one of the Cirque de Gavarnie in the Pyrenees. We followed the course of Pine Creek almost to its sources. It is a wild and beautiful stream; happily much of the old pine timber is still standing, although not nearly as much as in the days when Artist Shearer painted his masterpieces along its rocky banks.

At Eckville, or, freely translated, Pointville, we turned to the left, towards the majestic Pinnacle, whose slopes we would cross. We paused at a ruined stone house, the last building before reaching the mountain, as it possessed considerable interest to us. In the old days, it had been the home of Noah Hallman, called by his friends "Ark," a veteran of the Mexican War of 1847. The old fellow had learned the art of rope-throwing

34. Most likely over what is now Hawk Mountain Road.

in Texas or Mexico and kept himself in training in a unique way. Up on the headwaters of the Lehigh River, he captured four young Pennsylvania lions, or panthers. These he brought to his Berks County home and tamed. He would let them loose and send his dogs after them. When the hounds brought them to bay, he would lasso the ''painters" and drag them home. The sagacious brutes soon became used to the trick and enjoyed the chase as much as did dogs or huntsmen.[35]

At the barn nearest the Hallman ruins, eight woodchuck hides were nailed to the side of the barn, pitiful examples of the ''game" which now attracts the attention of full-grown, supposedly red-blooded Pennsylvania hunters.

Before long, we were in the depths of the grand forest that covers much of the sides of the Pinnacle. Here it was that we heard the mournful note of the dove, or "rainbird," a-coo, coo, coo, the first on this drive. The road was rough, but we did not mind, as the glory of the laurel, coming into full bloom on every side, was enough to send anyone into ecstasy. We stopped at an old turkey blind where some hunter had doubtless waited for the birds to pass; climbing up into it, we felt something of the thrill which every sportsman experiences as he enters the haunts of the game. Of course, we stopped at the Panther Spring, near where, in August 1874, two coal burners, Thomas Anson and Jacob Pfleger, had killed a mammoth Pennsylvania lion. The animal was first observed in Indiantown Gap, near Jonestown, and a party of thirty hunters went in pursuit. It eluded them, however, only to be brought to earth by the two intrepid nimrods of the Pinnacle.[36]

The road up the mountain was very steep; the timber was nearly all gone at the top, little else was growing except sweet fern and ripening huckleberries. To the north and west grand views opened out, of mountains, forests, remote valleys, and tiny, secluded farms. Once a ruffed grouse ran before our horses, and we heard the shrill, doleful cry of several blue jays. It was warm out there in the sun, but we plodded away until

35. Noah "Ark" Hallman, the Mexican War veteran may be an invention of Shoemaker. Oddly, there are no obvious records of this person and Shoemaker does not include Hallman in his *Pennsylvania Wild Cats* book published the following year.

36. This is the panther allegedly acquired by Shoemaker in 1912 and displayed in his study. Later research by Bradley Smith caught Shoemaker in a fib. According to Smith, while the story of the Anson/Pfleger panther is most likely true, the panther acquired by Shoemaker and displayed for years in his study is a different specimen.

we plunged into the forest again, where the road turns down towards Windsor Furnace. We were thirsty and hot, consequently hailed with delight the roar of a mountain stream, Windsor Brook, which presently greeted our ears.

We drove into the site of an abandoned hunter's camp and made preparations for our mid-day meal. We refreshed ourselves at the torrent, the water of which was so cold that it chilled our fingers. It flows like a jet from the very heart of the Pinnacle. It was near this stream that an Indian who kidnapped a white girl in the early days of Berks County, and held her prisoner on the mountain until she died of grief, was captured by her avenging lover and buried alive in its bed, so that only the top of his head appeared.[37] Today one can see the skull, with the broad brow and the shock of coarse, black hair, in the bed of the torrent, the cold water having seemingly kept this hideous "memento" intact.

We enjoyed our "picnic" immensely. The crackling fire looked well with its forest background; everything was cooked to a nicety. After lingering and dreaming for an hour or two after the repast, listening to the brook, the birds, the happy hum of our own conscience, we reluctantly started down the mountain. We passed the ruins of the old furnace,[38] once one of the leading industries of the northern end of the county, but enjoying most the waterfall from a rhododendron glen just above it.

We drove by the new reservoir,[39] which is supplying Hamburg with the icy cold Windsor Brook water, and came out on the public road near an old stone church. Out in the open country, we could admire the Blue Mountains in all their grandeur, their air of vastness, their sweeps of immense distance deeply impressing us.

From the highway, we obtained an excellent view of the new State Tuberculosis Sanitarium.[40] Surely it is an inspired spot for the location of a fort to fight the "great white plague." Before long we were in the neat town of Hamburg, "fairest village on the plain." We have always loved

37. This is a local legend, not historical fact.

38. The ruins of the Windsor Furnace (also known as the Windsor Iron Furnace) are located in Windsor Township, Berks County, near the base of the Blue Mountain. The forge that became Windsor Furnace was sold in 1768 to Jacob Winey of Philadelphia. It functioned as a charcoal-fueled blast furnace, producing cast iron through the mid-19th century. It was briefly abandoned around 1850 but rebuilt after the American Civil War. It went "out of blast" and permanently closed in 1882.

39. Most likely on what is now Reservoir Road and then Mountain Road.

40. Built 1914.

this simple, thriving, happy metropolis of northern Berks, and never did it look neater, or livelier, than in the clear light of this June afternoon.

We called and paid our respects to Editor W. O. Heinly,[41] who publishes the *Item*, a bright, newsy sheet, and he presented us with a photograph of the Blue Rocks, a great natural wonder located about four miles east of the town, at the foot of the mountain, where there is a field of some hundreds of acres of huge broken stones, beneath which can be heard the rumble of a subterranean stream.

Above "the rocks," near the mountain's comb, is Point Lookout, and a short distance to the west lies a large Indian burial ground. Points of interest are not lacking in the environs of "happy, prosperous" Hamburg. Before leaving the town, we took a look at the new post office building, where our good friend Abel H. Byers[42] holds forth to the eminent satisfaction of Uncle Sam, who is soon to make it a second-class office. Then we crossed the Schuylkill, on the old, covered bridge, pausing for a moment to admire the curious wooden weather vanes on the old bridge-tender's house. Two vanes, painted to resemble acrobats, a boy and a girl, swing Indian clubs, while a third, resembling a sailor man, leaning jealously near the girlish figure, is turning a wheel. These figures have inspired at least one story.

We followed the mountain road towards Shartlesville. At Seyfert's Mill,[43] with the date 1840 on it, there is a signboard pointing towards the mountain which says: "To Schuylkill Haven, 11 mi." There is an air of wildness, of bleakness, about the mountain road, and the swift-flowing Northkill, and the old stone mill, that have always thrilled us. We should love to follow that road some windy afternoon in autumn, when the jays were calling, the gum trees' leaves were red, and the sky gray and threatening.

The approach to Shartlesville is very beautiful. The town is bowered in trees, and is grouped like some old French fortress town, about a hill, on the top of which rises the ancient church, with its square brick tower.

41. William O. Heinly (July 10, 1863-December 29, 1931) owned the *Hamburg Item* from1887 until his death.

42. Abel Henry Byers (1856-1936) was the postmaster at Hamburg from 1898 (appointed by William McKinley) until he retired in 1915.

43. Seyfert Mill is a historic grist mill located in Upper Tulpehocken Township, Berks County, at the junction of Old U.S. Route 22 and Campsite Road. The combined mill and house building was built in 1840, and is a 2 1/2-story, with basement, banked stone building. It measures 48 by 50 feet (15 by 15 m). Also on the property are the contributing millrace and pond. The mill ceased operation in about 1954.

We have seen this tower on a night when the new horned-moon was behind it, shining through the mullioned belfry, and we thought of those words of Thomas Gray, "Within yon ivy mantled tower, the mournful owl doth to the moon complain."[44] This evening, in the soft light of the golden hour, it was equally and rapturously beautiful.

44. "Elegy Written in a Country Churchyard" was published in 1751.

THE PINNACLE

THE BLUE ROCKS (Great National Wonder Near Hamburg, Pa.)

Arrived Strausstown

Fine drive along "mountain road" to Shartlesville from Hamburg. Passed near site of Fort Northkill.

7:30 P.M.

EVENING was settling fast as we turned into the road below the sadly remodeled church at Strausstown, which leads to the site of Fort Northkill, of French and Indian War fame—and Degler's. The old church has been cruelly marred and seems to be trying to hide its face behind the hue grove of pines, hemlocks and oaks which grow along the ridge on which it stands. The Degler home is one of the very remarkable old houses of Berks County.[45] Below the gable is an iron plate on which is painted "1755-1886." This means that the original log cabin, built in 1755, was enlarged and weatherboarded at the latter date. In the attic is the celebrated chest, broken open by Indians in 1757. Just as the savages were stooping down to remove the treasure, they were shot dead by members of the Degler family. The chest is unpainted, and made of cedar wood, and, considering its age, is in an excellent state of preservation. On the broken lid are carved two hearts, with the initials "G. F. D." in the center, the date "1757" below. On the left of this are two lishes,[46] crossed, on the right two Indian clubs, crossed. The chest is held together by wooden nails. It has a curious old iron lock.

After inspecting this strange relic which is now owned by John W. Henne,[47] who married a relative of the Degler family. We strolled across the cornfield to the spring where Nicholas Long's home had been located, and where some Indian atrocities occurred. On the way, one of Mr. Henne's relatives, a boy named John F. Noecker, picked up a

45. The Degler home is referenced in historical accounts of the 1757 Bloody Springs massacre, where Lenape Indians attacked the home after the attack on the Spatz family near Strausstown.

46. Ropes.

47. John William Henne (April 26, 1883 – February 6, 1919) died during the Flu Epidemic. He was married to Maggie S. Long.

Howitzer ball and several arrow points. These, he said, were frequently found in all parts of the farm.

After drinking from the "bloody spring," we retraced our steps to the Degler home and were presented to Mrs. Sarah Noecker,[48] 73 years old, a daughter of the late John W. Degler,[49] the former owner of the property, who had been born in the historic old house. The old lady said that she had heard many Indian stories from her parents and the old people of the neighborhood when she was a young girl.

The sun was now gone behind the Blue Mountain, but an afterglow of cerise and crimson bespread the evening sky. The somber heights where once the carnage and tragedy of the natives held sway were bathed in the dark shadows of peaceful night. It was with many thoughts of the past that we were driven towards the ancient village of Strausstown.[50]

It was after suppertime when we drove up in front of the hotel,[51] but the landlord, Harry Paul,[52] smilingly declared that we could not arrive too late to be served. Mr. Paul, who is descended from one of the old French Huguenot families of Berks County, has all the suavity and courtesy of his race. He made our sojourn most enjoyable, and at the last minute before our departure, handed us a newly-arrived Philadelphia newspaper, so that we could read how the Britishers had won the final game in the International Polo Match.

48. She lived from 1843 to 1923. The boy, John F. Noecker, is likely a grandson or great-grandson.

49. He lived from 1821 to 1887.

50. Today, Bloody Spring Road, northwest of Shartlesville, wends its way to Strausstown if you follow it west.

51. Undoubtedly, the historic Center Hotel in Strausstown.

52. Harry Jacob Paul (November 28, 1875-February 6, 1927), a veteran of the Spanish-American War, was a native of Shartlesville, now buried at Zion Church Cemetery in Strausstown. He ran the Center Hotel for five years as well as a coal washery in Schuylkill County. For ten years, he was the Justice of the Peace at Strausstown. He died while running for County Commissioner. He was a son of John Albert Paul (1841-1920), a Civil War veteran who served in the 50th Pennsylvania.

READY TO START AT STRAUSSTOWN

Left Strausstown

Visited Fort Dietrich Snyder; good road across Blue Mountain.

June 18, 6:30 A.M.

IT was a bright, clear morning when we departed for Schubert, which lies at the foot of the Blue Mountain.[53] On the way we passed through a magnificent grove of original white oaks, the finest grove we had seen in Berks County, and doubtless one of the finest in the state. We rested and watered our horses at the Seven Stars Hotel[54] before beginning the steep climb to the site of Fort Dietrich Snyder.[55] It was a steep tug for the animals, but for us it was delightful, as we got out and walked up the road, which was well shaded and the woods filled with the biggest and fullest blown clusters of laurel that we had yet seen. The rattle and splash of a mountain stream enlivened the morning stillness.

When we gained the mountaintop the horses struck a trot, and we were soon in sight of the old hotel,[56] once kept by Harry Nein,[57] which stands a hundred feet south of the site of the fort. Our zest at re-visiting this historic spot was somewhat dulled when we were informed in Strausstown that old Mrs. Nein, the landlord's widow, who for years had lived alone in the old tavern, had been removed to the county home. Two years before we had met her and she not only showed us the exact

53. Before the construction of I-78, Taubert Road connected to Schubert Road. Today, you must go north from Strausstown, over the highway, and then left on Schubert Road.

54. According to George M. Meiser IX, the most significant building in Schubert is the former Seven Stars Hotel. It sits on the southwest corner of the main intersection at 5898 Four Point Road. It was one of several hotels in the region known by that name.

55. The Shoemakers likely rode on what is now Old Mountain Road, uphill less than two miles. A marker for the fort is located along Route 183 near where the Appalachian Trail crosses the highway in Schuylkill County.

56. The old Blue Mountain Hotel is now a ruin about twenty yards from the location of Fort Dietrich Snyder.

57. Neither Harry Nein nor his widow could found in the records. It would be difficult for a widow to live a lone atop the mountain. These might be fictional characters.

location of the fort, but the spring where Dolly Hope,[58] the wife of Captain Snyder, had washed her clothes. The Widow Nein's mother had been Dolly Snyder's servant, and she had been present when, in 1810, the old fort was torn down to be replaced by the present hotel structure.[59] Across the road is the signboard which reads: "Blue Mountain Hotel, 1784." There is probably no older hotel stand in Berks County. It was used as an inn from 1781 to about 1904, a period of one hundred and twenty years. Until 1810, the old fort was used as a hotel, but it became too small to accommodate the heavy travel that streamed across the mountain to and from Pottsville.

Dolly Snyder, the commandant's widow, lived to be 115 years of age,[60] and when she died, Mrs. Nein averred she was buried in the graveyard of Christ Lutheran Church at Stouchsburg, near the tomb of her lifelong friend, the celebrated Regina Hartman.[61] Dolly Snyder, it would appear, was an Englishwoman of quality, very beautiful and cultured, but how she became the wife of a hardy frontiersman, or came to live at this remote spot, remains one of the riddles of history.

Now the old hotel stands deserted and melancholy, the abode of ghosts and memories of other days. What scenes this mountaintop has witnessed—Indian forays, ambuscades, hunting escapades, the long lines of pioneers and packers bound for the regions beyond the mountains, love, hate, drunkenness, storm, sunshine, and, lastly, shadow. We walked about the deserted structure, and were seized with a desire to enter. Within was that musty odor so characteristic of all empty houses; it is the odor of bones, where the spirit is no more. We visited the tiny sample-room, where we could picture even Indians, as well as stalwart hunters, pioneers, teamsters, mysterious strangers and the like leaning on

58. This appears to be a snippet from "A Story of Regina: Another Fragment of the Popular Legend" included in the book *Black Forest Souvenirs*, published in 1914. This story would have been fresh in Henry Shoemaker's mind, having worked on that book in the months prior to this trip into the Blue Mountains.

59. How would Shoemaker know of these connections?

60. It is very unlikely Dolly Hope Snyder lived to be 115.

61. Regina Hartman Leininger (born 1746) is buried at Christ Lutheran Church Cemetery in Stouchsburg. She was taken during the Indian troubles as a child, during the Penn's Creek Massacre near Selinsgrove, along with another girl from her neighborhood. She lived amongst the natives for nearly nine years until arrangements were made by Colonel Bouquet to return all captives to their original families. Many came from all over the state. Her mother searched and searched but was unable to find her daughter, who by now, was much older and no longer spoke any German. It was suggested to her mother to sing a German hymn which the child might remember. The song alone yet not alone am I is a very solemn, unique song with an unusual tone. When her mother started to sing, in German, the girl stepped out from among the crowd of captives and started to sing along. Mother and daughter united again.

the bar. We went upstairs into the little rooms where all kinds of travelers with all kinds of stories had slept. Oh, to have been able to know their thoughts! We looked out of the attic window, where the cool breeze was swaying the leaves of the old horse chestnut trees. An oriole or "golden robin" had its nest so near that we could have reached it if we cared to, a beautifully woven hanging nest. We came downstairs and out into the sweet sunshine, so different from the mustiness and gloom of that ghostly house.

Before we left, we plucked a red rose from an ancient bush, no doubt planted by the rare Dolly Snyder herself. It was almost as if we had stepped into the past, or seen ghosts; we felt so oppressed as we drove down the steep road towards Snyder Valley, in Schuylkill County. Crossing the road was a large land turtle, which we captured, carving our initials and the date 1914 on the bottom of the shell. This creature, dull of wits and slow of motion, possessed the potentiality for a long life, and would be found and our identity wondered at long after we were no more.

Snyder Valley is wild and beautiful. It was subdued for settlement by Dietrich Snyder after many fierce encounters with the Indians and has ever since borne the name of its pacifier. We came to a cool spot by a small creek, and there another dinner was prepared. As a sample of our menus, let it be said that we had fried beefsteak, fried potatoes with onions, beans, toast, coffee, oranges, cake and cheese. What could be better than that as a mid-day repast for mountain climbers? We rested and meditated after the meal, watching several buzzards soaring far above us. Evidently, they had scented a feast on the offal of our picnic.

We continued our way to Friedensburg,[62] where we made inquiry as to the location of the Falls of the Swatara,[63] which rose near there. No one knew. We had seen a picture and read a description of the falls in a *Pictorial History of Pennsylvania* by Eli Bowen, published in 1852,[64] so surely they must exist somewhere.

62. A ride of about 5 or 6 miles from the mountaintop.

63. The Falls of the Swatara are located near Tremont, in Schuylkill County. It is a scenic 25-foot waterfall with a gorge, large boulders, and rhododendron, but now has graffiti and mine drainage issues. It is no longer open to the public; it's located on private property, and access is blocked.

64. The actual title is *The Pictorial Sketch Book of Pennsylvania*.

We drove to Panther Valley, where the stream heads in the Second Mountain, meeting an intelligent woman, Mrs. Annie Reiland,[65] who resided near Cressona. She said that she had never heard of the Falls, but would ask her father-in-law, Albanus Reiland,[66] ninety years old, who had lived in the valley nearly all his life, if he knew of this natural beauty spot. The old gentleman, who is the oldest active Sunday School teacher in Pennsylvania, said that he was aware of no Falls, except that the stream tumbled over the rocks as it emerged from the mountain, a mile to the north.[67]

We drove in that direction, passing the home of Mrs. Kate Reiland,[68] known as the greatest waffle-baker in Pennsylvania, and who has entertained celebrities from Wilkes-Barre, Scranton, New York, Philadelphia, and Pittsburgh with her renowned chicken and waffle suppers. But we found no Falls, though we traced the Swatara, which, by the way, is spelled in this valley "Swetara," almost to its source. We would have gone to the very beginning, only the thickets were so dense.

Somewhat disappointed, we turned our horses' heads towards Pine Grove, the grand old tannery town. We drove down the "mountain road," in preference to the "valley road," as it was wilder.[69] As the afternoon progressed, we heard the "bob-white" of many quails, the sharp cheep of snipe, the mournful of the killdeer.

65. Annie could not be located but her last name was likely spelled Ryland, similarly to others in the cemetery.

66. Albanus S. Riland (December 22, 1824 – March 21, 1921) lived near Friedensburg. He is buried in the St. John's Reformed Church there.

67. Mr. and Mrs. Shoemaker rode in the wrong direction to find the falls.

68. A Kathryn Straub Riland (November 7, 1873 – January 1, 1956) was married to Samuel Burkhart Riland, a nephew of Albanus Riland. Her obituary did not report her prowess with waffles.

69. This was likely a ride of about 11 miles.

OLD SIGNBOARD AT FORT DIETRICH SNYDER

Arrived Pine Grove

Quaint old town; Filbert House good.

6:30 P.M.

AGAIN, it was past supper time when we readied our destination. But the landlord[70] of the Filbert House,[71] where we stopped, courteously received us, and we were soon provided for in that respect. The old town, with its commodious homes and magnificent shade trees, never looked lovelier.

70. Charles Milton Yocum (1871-1956) was likely the proprietor at this time. He was born in Pine Grove Township. He learned telegraphing, is married to a Miss Zimmerman, has one son Slater, and one daughter Joyce, who is a stenographer and typewriter. He has kept the Filbert House for 15 years. He owns the property.

71. The Pine Grove Hotel, now the Filbert House, was kept by Israel Reinhard in 1841 and by the following others up to the present time (1916): Samuel Reinhard, D. Fessig, Philip Koons, J. Connoly, Samuel Miller, Samuel Filbert, Milton Ludwig, M. Relchendorf, William Tallman, Wm. Reed, Charles Yocum.

We strolled down the street in the cool of the evening, to pay our respects to Messrs. Anderson[72] and Reber,[73] who publish that interesting newspaper, the *Pine Grove Herald*. We found the two gentlemen in their office, also our old friend, the former proprietor of the paper, Mr. Gilbert.[74] It was a delightful evening, spent in congenial company, and the hour was late when we started back to our hotel.

---

72. Charles F. Anderson was born at Port Royal, Juniata Co., May 9th, 1870, came to Pine Grove Feb. 21st, 1891, is a printer by trade, worked on the *Pine Grove Herald* for some 20 years, then in partnership with Mr. H. F. Reber bought the *Herald* Dec. 1, 1909. Mr. Anderson is married to Lillie Irene Filbert; they have two sons and two daughters. Howard F. is clerk in Harrisburg; Paul is learning telegraphy; Mary E. and Ellen E. are at home.

73. Horace F. Reber is the only son of Mr. and Mrs. Franklin W. Reber and was born at Rock, Washington Township, on February 25, 1866. In 1880, the family moved to town (Pine Grove) where he attended the public schools, graduating from the High School in 1885. He was for a short time employed at the Gensemer Brothers tannery, and in October of 1885, he entered the employ of the Philadelphia & Reading Railway as a clerk in the scale office where S. M. Helms, now of Reading, was the weighmaster. On January 1, 1894, he entered the Country Commissioners' office as second assistant clerk, on January 1 he was promoted to first assistant clerk, and on January 1, 1897, he was promoted to Chief Clerk succeeding Phil. J. Connell. In 1899 he became a candidate for County Commissioner and was elected over Frank J. Brennan, of Shenandoah, having the highest vote for that office. He was re-elected in the fall of 1892 for a second term, completing a continuous twelve-year service in that important office. in 1897 he was wedded to Ella R. Hoffman, of Tower City. The family having six children as follows: Florence, teaching in the public schools of Schuylkill Haven; Norman D., chief clerk in the Gensemer & Salen tannery offices; Ferd. L., resort solicitor for the Philadelphia Record; Harold M., bookkeeper for Simon & Sherman, slaughters of Reading; Esther E., employed as file clerk in the Health Department at Harrisburg, and Dorothy at home. The six children with the father graduated from the local High school. Mr. Reber became a member of Company G, Fourth Infantry, N. G. P., for eight years, attaining the rank of Second Lieutenant, the Company then under the command of Capt. James W. Umbenhauer. In 1906, he started a hosiery mill operating by electric light, being the first electrically lighted plant in the town. He also operated the first washery in the Swatara Creek run by gasoline power. He sold out his interest in the stocking plant to his partner, John E. Reber, of Pottsville, and on Dec. 1, 1909, became associated with C. F. Anderson in conducting the *Pine Grove Herald*, a weekly paper, being engaged in that business together with reportorial work at the present time. He served in the local borough council and the school board for several times, serving at present as secretary and member of the board. He is a member of Camp 49, P. O. S. of A., and Pine Grove Castle, No. 124, Knights of the Golden Eagle, in which he has served as trustee for more than fifteen years.

74. Alfred Gilbert was born in Lykens Valley Sept. 9th, 1849, on a farm, was educated in the common schools of Washington Township of Dauphin Co. and the Berrysburg Seminary; was apprentice to Israel Reed, carpenter and contractor, and worked at the trade four years, then learned photography with Samuel Miller, of Lykens, and opened a gallery in Pine Grove in 1872. Successfully pursuing this line of business in connection with a job printing plant until 1878, when he sold the photography outfit and founded the *Pine Grove Herald*. The first copy was issued Dec. 14, 1878. He bought the first font of type and erected the first printing press in this Borough. He successfully published the *Herald* for 31 years, when on Dec. 1, 1909, he sold the plant and goodwill to the present owners, Anderson & Reber. He is connected fraternally with the Odd Fellows Lodge, and served three years as District Deputy Grand Master; was nine years treasurer of Pine Grove Castle No. 124, K. G. E., and a charter member. Also a prominent Mason of Pine Grove Lodge No. 409, having passed the chairs in 1894; recently receiving as a present from the local lodge a Past Master's Jewel for meritorious work. On Dec. 24th, 1872, he was married to Elizabeth Shaud, of Jonestown, Lebanon County. He has always taken an interest in the welfare of his adopted town and was a strong advocate in securing water in this Borough, and permanent good roads; was one of the first men in securing a National Bank charter and has been one of the directors of the board since its institution in this town in 1906.

Left Pine Grove

Picturesque road from Suedberg to Inwood, along mountain. St. Joseph's Well, and Cold Spring, well worth a visit.

June 19, 7:00 A.M.

EARLY the next morning, we were on our way, bound for Suedberg.[75] The road led along the side of the Blue Mountain, with the Swatara, stained black with the dust from the coal mines, flowing below us. We noticed many wild flowers in the rich, dark woods. The laurel was everywhere, but not quite in full bloom. There were many huge rhododendron trees covered with buds. These would bloom in the last days of June. We saw much rattlesnake weed, sweet pepper bush, evening primrose, harebell, wild roses, yarrow, Solomon's seal, pink fireweed, as well as the large magenta-hued blossoms of the dish-berry. A ruffed grouse ran in front of the horses, seeming loath to dart into the bushes; also, several rabbits, which twitched their delicate noses as we passed.

Towards noon, we came into the majestic Swatara Gap. Here, the mountains seem sky high, and the creek widens into the proportions of a river. Most authorities state that the name Swatara is of Indian origin, but the old Scotch-Irish families living near its confluence with the Susquehanna at Middletown declare that it is named for a stream in the North of Ireland, in Derry, called the Swatragh. In Pennsylvania, this name has been changed to Swatara, Swetara, Sewataro, and other variations.

At Inwood,[76] we crossed the stream and returned through the Gap in the direction of Tomstown.[77] Noticing a small crossroads store advertising ice cream, we purchased some, which we took with us for our dinner.

75. About three miles west of Pine Grove.

76. About six miles Suedberg.

77. About three miles from Inwood, back through the pass, to Tomstown, along what is now Tomstown Road.

The road now led into wild mountains, where primitive looking log cabins were the only sign of habitation. In the wildest part of one of the ravines, we met a slim, blonde girl of perhaps nine or ten years of age, a modern prototype of Regina Hartman, herding a number of cows. She carried a small lunch basket and probably remained in those mountains, rain or shine, from dawn to dark every day. We gave her an orange, and she directed us to the shortest way to St. Joseph's Well. The "well" proper gushes out of the rocks, being curiously walled up, beneath the shade of four giant white pines. The water flows through a springhouse and into Indiantown Run.[78]

We pitched our camp for lunch on the spot, as we afterwards learned, where the old hermit, Joseph Raber, was murdered by drowning in December 1878. Several rough characters residing in the mountains insured his life in their favor for a large amount and then pushed him from a log on which he was crossing the creek, holding him under the water until he was dead. For this dastardly crime, five men were hanged.[79]

In recent years, Pottsville residents have established a hunting lodge near the well, but in some way incurred the hatred of the mountaineers to such an extent that three successive cottages have been burned down by unknown incendiaries. It was a quaint spot, under the grand old forest trees, and we enjoyed it despite the depressing associations.

After dinner, we drove further into the mountains, in Fishing Creek Valley, in the direction of Cold Spring. On one of the high points where we could see Indiantown Gap and Manada Gap, and where the dwarfed jack pines rattled in the storm wind, we came upon a tiny cabin built of logs and mud. Nearby was a log barn, with a straw or thatched roof. Kneeling in the garden, pulling weeds, was the old recluse of the Second Mountain, Joseph Ney.[80] The aged man greeted us genially, and we complimented him upon the excellent manner in which he carried his eighty-four years. He told us that he lived alone, save for his faithful dog Wasser, which snapped and snarled as we drew near the slab fence surrounding the garden. He said that there were still a number of wildcats in the surrounding mountains, but they did no harm, also foxes, raccoons,

78. Through Indiantown Gap.

79. The perpetrators were famously known at the time as the "Blue-Eyed Six."

80. This is most likely the Civil War veteran Joseph Z. Ney (February 2, 1831 to November 13, 1924). According to his obituary, his wife had died around 1899, coinciding with his move to the mountains. Ney is buried in Schuylkill Haven Union Cemetery.

skunks, possums, hawks, and wild turkeys. Twenty-five years ago, when he had first moved to his eyrie, black bears came into his fields.

As we drove on, we wondered what was the life story of this hermit, what romance or blighted wish drove him into this forest cloister. The pull up the mountain was a severe one, but the view from the summit, a sylvan panorama in all directions, justified the effort. At length, we reached the famed Cold Spring in Stony Creek Valley.[81] The old hotel, a popular resort a quarter of a century ago, was burned to the ground, and a YMCA Camp has risen in its stead. The spring bubbles out of a bed of yellow sand, and is now covered by a spring house of tasteful design. Above the spring stand three original white pine trees, monarchs of the forest, trees that surely saw the Indians. There is the stump of a fourth pine, but it was probably broken down in some storm. All about are fine oaks and chestnuts, making an ideal picnic or camping ground.

81. Northern end of Lebanon County.

Arrived Grantville

Hotel keeper at Grantville anxious to please.

7:30 P.M.

WE had passed many picnic groves on our trip, but none of them had water handy, which to us seemed very strange. No wonder that the park at Cold Spring enjoys such widespread popularity, for never was better water tasted by mankind. About a mile away is a fine lake,[82] caused by damming up a creek, and several rowboats were moored on it. Under the stormy sky, it was like some Adirondack pond; snipe were skimming over its surface. The sky was very dark, but the storm held off until we were back in the Valley of Fishing Creek. Then came thunder and lightning, the heavens literally opened, and we were drenched before we could adjust the side curtains. The storm approached oddly enough. Once the rain was coming down on the far side of a field which adjoined the road, while on the road where we were, it was perfectly dry.

The shower, severe though it was, was over before we reached Manada Gap. Streaks of clear, silvery sky appeared; there were traces of the sunset behind the uneven ridges of the Second Mountain. We drove through the Gap, which reminded us much of the beautiful Delaware Gap near Thompsontown, in Juniata County, and thence to Grantville, where we put up for the night at a comfortable inn.[83]

The next morning was clear and cool, ideal weather for an early start. Professor E. E. Lerch,[84] the local school teacher, kindly consented to accompany us to the old Presbyterian burying-ground at West Hanover[85] and to the site of Fort Brown. In the cemetery are many ancient

82. Possibly the DeHart Reservoir.

83. The Old Grantville Hotel.

84. Elsworth Aldo Lerch (June 24, 1861 – August 9, 1939) is buried at Saint John's United Methodist Church Cemetery in Grantville. He was a teacher at East Hanover Township for fifty years.

85. The Old Hanover Presbyterian Churchyard is located at 1477 Ridge Rd, Grantville, PA 17028.

tombstones, including those of the celebrated Col. William Allen, son of the founder of Allentown, and himself a leader in the French and Indian War, who died on October 16, 1794, aged 51 years. Nearby is the modest tombstone erected to the memory of John Craig and wife, who were killed by Indians in a lane not far away on October 22, 1756. Souvenir hunters have seriously damaged this stone. There is also a monument erected to John Hampton, who died in 1900, at the age of 100 years. Until a few months before his death, he walked twice every week to Harrisburg and back, to market, carrying two heavy baskets. His mind was unimpaired to the last, and in 1894, he was a valued aid to Mr. H. M. M. Richards,[86] of Reading, in locating Manada Fort for the Pennsylvania State Historical Commission. We saw monuments belonging to the McCreight, McCormick, Snodgrass, Gilbert, Lamberton, Boyer and other families, well-known today in and about Harrisburg. Outside the stone wall of God's Acre are the modest graves of the slaves.[87] The old Presbyterian Church was torn down by ruthless innovators a number of years ago.

While we were in the graveyard, a night-hawk or bull bat flew up from a marble slab and winged his way in a dazed sort of way to a branch in an acacia tree. The first settlers had droll names for the beasts and birds; the night hawk, a dusk flyer and heavy of wing, was called the bull bat, while the huge water wader, the great blue heron, was given the name of gander snipe. The short-tailed bay lynx was called the bobcat!

86. Henry Melchior Muhlenberg Richards (August 16, 1848 – September 28, 1935) was an American military officer who served in the Union Army during the American Civil War and then as a captain in the United States Navy during the Spanish–American War. He was a member of the Muhlenberg family, a United States political, religious, and military dynasty based in the state of Pennsylvania. Muhlenberg College in Allentown, Pennsylvania, is named in the family's honor. (Wikipedia)

87. There are estimates of 150 slave graves: 100 outside the wall and 50 inside. All the graves are unmarked.

GRANTVILLE

HENRY MELCHIOR MUHLENBERG RICHARDS

Left Grantville

West Hanover Presbyterian Graveyard, and sites of Manada Fort and Fort Brown well worth visiting, also mountain road to Beelzebub. Passed through Jonestown, a fine old-time town.

June 20, 6:30 A.M.

FROM West Hanover graveyard, we drove to the ruins of Fort Brown.[88] This building stood on the Ramler property and was torn down about twenty-five years ago. The Historical Commission, which did so much to rescue the sites from oblivion, was appointed ten years too late to save most of the structures themselves. Mr. Ramler owns a tract of several hundred acres of virgin oak timber along the slope of the Blue Mountain, and we followed the mountain road, so as to see it, passing through the little village of Beelzebub, where Joe Moonshine keeps store.[89]

In this village, we met a man named Rhoads,[90] who showed us a huge Indian war hammer which he had lately unearthed on his farm. From Beelzebub we drove through Lemberger's, and then in the direction of Indiantown Gap.[91] The thought of this Gap evoked many memories, among them the legend of a lynx, or catamount, that we once heard, which sprang in front of a runaway horse, stopping it and saving the driver's life. Later, when the lynx was killed by some bounty hunters, the man whose life it had saved bought the carcass, had it stuffed and set it up in a glass case on his porch.

---

88. Today, the site is near the Manada Golf Club.

89. This is a 19th century legend.

90. There are several Rhoads men buried in Shellsville.

91. Beelzebub might have been close to the current Hollywood Casino. Lemberger's currently is a small cemetery and church close to Harper Tavern, at the intersection of Harrison School Road and Mill Road. The village there now abuts Interstate 81 on the north.

At the entrance to the Gap we stopped to talk with old Joe Schmeader,[92] a basket maker, who sat under a big ash tree weaving his wares from strips of Welsh willow. We bought two baskets, as souvenirs of a trade which is fast passing away. Gone are most of the old generation of basket-makers, carpet weavers, umbrella menders, watch repairers, tinkers and peddlers, who traveled from farm to farm.

The papers only a few days ago, recorded the passing, at the age of 76, of Charles Zimmerman, who for fifty years drew a little hand wagon through the remoter sections of Berks County, fixing watches, clocks and doing other useful tasks.[93] While we were discussing the old days with the picturesque basketmaker, Gipsy Bill,[94] a noted horse trader, his wife, and son came along. They said that times had changed, that horse-trading wasn't what it used to be. Horses were scarcer, and their owners were less willing to part with them.

Further on in the (Indiantown) Gap, which is wild and romantic, we stopped to meet the hoary patriarch, John Trout,[95] who has lived in the Gap for seventy of his eighty-two years. He said that wolves were fairly numerous when he moved there in 1844, and that a panther had been killed in the Gap as late as 1830. Catamounts were gone, but wildcats were still to be found, and bear tracks had been observed the previous winter. A bear had been actually killed in 1913 on the Second Mountain, the first in that region in many years.

We cooked our mid-day meal in a cool, sequestered spot, near a spring, the *pièce de résistance* being boiled new potatoes, and then set out for Jonestown. We reached that interesting old community in the mid-afternoon. We met the local fire engine on the bridge that crosses the Swatara; it was not going to a fire, but was being used to advertise an ice cream festival. At Heilman's hotel, in the big square, we watered our thirsty horses. The old town had changed little since we were last there, several years ago. The Golden Stag and the White Horse, the two oldest

92. This individual could not be located. Perhaps he was an itinerant.

93. Charles Zimmerman (May 22, 1838 – June 13, 1914) was buried at the Berks County Almshouse Cemetery. According to FindaGrave: "married, watchmaker, born Germany, died at county almshouse, remains sent for anatomical research, as done with most German-born males who died here."

94. This individual could not be located.

95. John Trout (February 18, 1833 – March 10, 1923) was a Civil War veteran who lived his entire life in the Indiantown Gap. In his younger days, he was a trapper. Later, he was a small-scale farmer and huckster. His obituary described him as one of the oldest and "most picturesque" residents of Lebanon County.

taverns, had been slightly remodeled, a new brick store building faced the open square, or marketplace, that was all.

At the Heilman House,[96] we met a Mr. D. C. Ney,[97] who proved to be a nephew of the old hermit of the Second Mountain, Joseph Ney. He said that his uncle had never been a hunter, but another uncle, Thomas Ney,[98] had been famed as a nimrod in the Blue Mountains. This old man, who died ten years ago in his 86th year,[99] had killed wolves in the Blue Mountains in his youth, also bears and deer. He had taken part in the unsuccessful panther chase of 1874, and in company with Bill Swoyer, another mighty hunter, had entered bear dens in Bear Rock, near Cold Spring, slaying the beasts in their lairs.[100] He told about Leonard Faler,[101] another hunter, who boasted that he never killed a bear outside of its den. Once, his son John shot a bear on the slope of the Third Mountain, and when the old man found it out, he said that he felt ashamed of the boy for his lack of courage, ordering him never to do it again. The wolves, it seemed, had a well-defined path along the Second Mountain as far as the Susquehanna, where it branched off towards the wilder regions of Clark's Creek Valley. Mr. Ney believed that Dr. Kalbfus,[102] of the State Game Commission, should liberate deer on the Blue Mountain between Swatara Gap and the Pinnacle, providing them with a five-year closed season until they felt at home. This sentiment had also been expressed by landlord Berk[103] at Steinsville, who said that the deer could have a magnificent range, and would be in that section now had they not been driven out by hunters with dogs before the game laws put a stop to this

96. The Heilman House Hotel (or Heilman Hotel) in Jonestown was a prominent 19th-century building on the square that served as a key community hub and the temporary home of the Jonestown Bank around 1880. Later associated with Spannuth's restaurant, it operated until the early 1950s and was later replaced by a laundromat.

97. Daniel C. Ney (April 1, 1857 – April 24, 1944) is buried in Zion Lutheran Cemetery in Jonestown. He was the son of Daniel Ney (1820-1903).

98. Thomas Ney (August 10, 1816 – September 18, 1891) is buried in Moonshine Cemetery in Jonestown.

99. The age and years do not match the Thomas Ney buried in Jonestown. Perhaps Shoemaker is fabricating this tale.

100. William H. Swoyer (May 9, 1860 – November 12, 1944) was born in Lancaster. He married Evenna M. Fleisher in Pine Grove in 1883, so he is possibly the Bill Swoyer mentioned. This Swoyer died near Scranton.

101. This individual could not be located.

102. Dr. Joseph Kalbfus (1852–1919) was a pioneering conservationist and the first Chief Game Protector/Secretary of the Pennsylvania Game Commission, serving from 1898 until his death in 1919. He was instrumental in establishing the state's game refuge system, promoting the 1913 resident hunter's license, and fighting for wildlife protection.

103. Daniel P. Berk mentioned earlier.

unsportsmanlike method of hunting. Mr. Berk stated that he had not seen deer tracks on the Pinnacle in twenty-five years.

From Jonestown we drove in the calm afternoon sunlight to the queer, old-fashioned town of Fredericksburg, which also has a square, or marketplace. Then we followed the mountain road[104] to the Half-Way House, where we branched off towards Millersburg,[105] through quaint Grindstone Valley.

On the road to the Half-Way House we obtained a fine view of the valleys, with Meckville[106] lying in the foreground. A stage, bound for Pine Grove, passed us. In the back seat sat a pretty bride, decked out with a veil and white dress, while the groom wore, as the country papers say, "a conventional black suit." We obtained a wonderful view of the Round Top, a high mountain, which in some places is unscalable, as we neared old Millersburg.

104. This would likely be the road headed to Pine Grove, which goes up and over the mountain. They would have then turned east along the base of the mountain, heading to Bethel.

105. Millersburg was renamed to Bethel. Shoemaker still refers to it as Millersburg.

106. Meckville is a village west of Bethel in Berks County.

HEILMAN HOUSE IN JONESTOWN

OLD SIGNBOARD AT JONESTOWN

Arrived Millersburg

*Fine scenery, quaint atmosphere, polite attention at Golden Eagle Hotel. Good roads all the way. Fort Henry near at*hand.

6:30 P.M.

THE sun was sinking low as we drove into the open square of the ancient town, continuing our way until we reached the Golden Eagle Hotel, kept by our old-time friend, Charles E. Kerr.[107] On a wire opposite was perched a snow-white robin, caroling gaily. We were so engrossed by it that we forgot to get out of the carriage until the landlord and his son Louis, a youth of artistic talents, greeted us familiarly. The old place seemed just the same, even to the giant Ailanthus trees which shaded roofs and porches. They were in full bloom now, exuding an odor not unlike that of the chestnut blossom. The old-fashioned garden at the house next door was as charming as of yore; there was much of an air of serenity and peace.

After supper we strolled down the road to an old Lutheran Church on the hill. In the quiet, grass-grown cemetery we gazed upon the bold, black outline of the distant Round Top, standing clear-cut and distinct against the steel gray evening sky. On either side of it stretched the seemingly limitless, endless ridges of the Kittochtinny range. It was in the cemetery that we experienced that sense of exaltation that brings us nearer to the Infinite. Such experiences are rare in this life!

We strolled back to the hotel, going by a farmhouse covered with honeysuckle vines which exuded the sweetest of perfumes. Many country boys were out driving their buggies, for it was on a Saturday night. Some had their sweethearts with them, others were on their way to meet them.

---

107. Charles E. Kurr (June 20, 1880 – November 23, 1918) lived and died in Bethel, Pennsylvania. The Louis who was mentioned could be his younger brother Lewis Bryan Kurr (1898-1978).

Over the back of the seat of every buggy hung a lap-robe ornamented with a gaily-colored floral design.

On the hotel porch, we met an old mountaineer named John Kline,[108] who told us many legends of long ago. One of them was of a lead mine, located somewhere in the Blue Mountains, perhaps near the Pine Garden. Indians trading with the white people sold much of this lead but steadfastly refused to reveal the whereabouts of the mine. They were on especially friendly terms with one old man, who begged them so hard to show him the mine that they consented. But they blindfolded him before leading him to the spot. When it was reached, after a long climb, the hoodwink was removed, and the sight which met his gaze was unforgettable. There seemed to be enough ore in sight to supply the nation. He tried to mark the locality in some way before his eyes were covered again. But he was never able to find the mine, though he searched the mountains for years.

Another story was of an old settler who, fearing an attack by Indians, hid a pot of gold on the mountain. The old man died before he could go after his treasure, but he gave the instructions to his son-in-law. This fellow could not locate it, nor could many others who went in search of it. One man eventually discovered it but swore an awful oath as he reached down to pick it up. The pot of gold disappeared before his eyes. No one has yet regained it.

The next morning, we saw the white robin attacked by three normal-colored robins and whirled about in the air until it screamed with pain. Louis told us that the bird had a mate of the ordinary hue and several young ones. His nest was in a horse-chestnut tree which had red blossoms—a rarity, as most trees of this kind have white blooms, though some are pink.

108. John H. Kline (July 29, 1855 – November 30, 1934) was a farmer. He was buried at Salem Reformed Church Cemetery in Bethel.

Left Millersburg

Picturesque drive to Rehrersburg and Stouchsburg, across hills; roads good. Tulpehocken Church; very interesting.

June 21, 8:00 A.M.

ACCOMPANIED by young Mr. Kerr, we drove out to call on old George Potts,[109] a Civil War veteran and noted as a hunter of wildcats. He lived alone on a lane a short distance beyond the site of Fort Henry, another important point in the bloody days of 1755-60. Old Mr. Potts, who is quite spry despite his seventy-three years, described to us how he had killed several large wildcats near his home. He said that these animals were still fairly numerous, but hard to catch, and that foxes were still quite plentiful. When he was a boy, sixty-five years ago, wolves were numerous in the Blue Mountain above his home; there were still a few when he returned from the war in 1864. A few years after the close of the war, Dan Long,[110] who lived at the foot of the mountain back of Livengood's Mill, had killed a brown wolf. He had seen the pelt, which was sold for ten dollars, and the scalp, on which five dollars was paid. It appeared that Long, who was a young man at the time, owned an unsexed female dog, which used to run off with the lone wolf and hunt with him for several days on the mountain. The wolf would wait for the dog in the evenings on a point of rocks in the glen, and one night Long slipped out and killed the monster. The dog was disconsolate for days. Oh, the sordid, terrible tragedies of animal as well as human life! On our way to Rehrersburg we passed the mill where the last wolf of the Blue Mountains was slain and felt a strong desire to seek out the rocky gorge where he met his end!

109. This individual could not be located.

110. Daniel B. Long (September 4, 1851 – November 27, 1923) is buried at Rehrersburg in the Altalaha Lutheran Cemetery. He would have been a teenager at the time described. Is this the Dan Long Shoemaker mentions?

We had dinner at Rehrersburg, at the Union House, where the landlord, Mr. G. R. Snyder,[111] and his wife, were very solicitous of our comfort.

Then we started across the hills for Stouchsburg, in hopes of finding some trace of the grave of Regina Hartman, "the Blue Mountain Captive." Every Pennsylvanian knows the story of Regina, how she, at the age of nine, was stolen by Indians from her parents' home in Orwigsburg,[112] in October, 1755, was kept a captive for nine years and was restored to her mother, out of a long line of released Indian prisoners at Carlisle, when the good woman, at the suggestion of Col. Bouquet, sang a song which she had heard in childhood. Modern research has shown that the girl to whom these adventures actually occurred was named Regina Leininger, and that she was captured on the Karoondinha,[113] in what is now Snyder County. But residents of Berks, Schuylkill, and Lebanon Counties will always believe that there was a Regina Hartman, of Orwigsburg, who was captured by Indians, was loved by one of them named Kaniserega, whom she refused to marry after her captivity was ended because her mother hated every member of the race that slew the others of the family. Later on, a white man, Anders Boon, of Exeter, loved her, but she spurned him because she still loved the Indian. She gave him a lock of her blonde hair in a thoughtless moment, and this Kaniserega found in a locket around the white lover's neck when he butchered him at the massacre of Fort Freeland, on the West Branch of the Susquehanna in July 1779. Our Regina, whom the Indians called "Rag-hena," never married, was noted for her saintliness and her charities, and when she died, her body was conveyed to the graveyard of the church where she worshiped, being interred with simple honors. No stone marks it, and even the exact location is unknown. The only key we had was what old Mrs. Nein had told us, "Regina lies beside her old friend Dolly Snyder."

On the road to the old Tulpehocken Church, we caught many fleeting glimpses of the Blue Mountains, so soon to be veiled from us. Birds of all kinds were in song, robins, brown thrushes, kingbirds, larks, and peewees. Above sailed the solemn and funereal turkey buzzards. Many wild

111. George R. Snyder (1873-1938) was born in Rehrersburg. His wife's name was Emma. They are buried in Charles Evans Cemetery in Reading.

112. Actually near Selinsgrove during the Penn's Creek Massacre.

113. Another name for Penn's Creek.

flowers and wild strawberries grew by the roadsides, very sweet-smelling; among the flowers were the evening primrose, the gay-colored butterfly-weed, butter and eggs, St. John's wort, elder blossoms, and milkweed blooms. Milkweed shoots, closely resembling asparagus, are stewed and eaten with relish by the Pennsylvania mountaineers in the early spring. We saw numerous butterflies that flitted gracefully about. We passed through many groves of stately rock oaks and white oaks, where there were considerable numbers of gray and red squirrels. Every "stone-row" had its quota of chipmunks.

In due course of time, we came in sight of the old stone church, which we recognized from the illustration of it in Reverend Weiser's story of Regina.[114] The forest which surrounded it in the holy days of the Reverend John Nicholas Kurtz[115] was no more, but a goodly grove stands in the foreground. We stopped with feelings of true reverence before this severe, solemn edifice, where the bold pioneers of generations long since gone worshiped. Christ Evangelical Lutheran Church—for that is its full appellation—was first erected in 1743. The first edifice was replaced by the present structure in 1786. This was partly destroyed by a premature explosion of dynamite in a quarry across the Harrisburg Pike in 1885, necessitating the construction of a new roof and a new interior. The foundations of the edifice of 1743 are to be seen in the road which divides the present church from the old graveyard. Reverend Kurtz, who confirmed Regina Hartman, was pastor of the church from 1748 to 1770.

Accompanied by the sexton, Mr. James Meredith,[116] we visited the interior of the church, which is plain but dignified. A fine painting of Christ praying in the wilderness adorns the wall in the back of the plain walnut pulpit. We then visited the two graveyards; the newest one is in the churchyard, the oldest one across the driveway. The sexton showed us where he thought Regina was probably buried, but that was all. It was left for us to conjecture.[117]

---

114. Reverend Clement Zwingli Weiser (1830-1898) was a classmate of Dr. Reuben H. Muth at Marshall College (see *A Saddlebag Doctor of the Mahantongo Valley*) who wrote an early biography of his great-grandfather, Conrad Weiser. In that book, he included the tale of Regina. Weiser had the Hartmans living near Fort Henry.

115. Kurtz (1722-1794) was the first Lutheran minister ordained in Pennsylvania.

116. Quite possibly this is actually John Henry Meredith (May 11, 1864 – July 9, 1939) who is buried at the church in Stouchsburg.

117. There is now a marker in the cemetery, though the actual grave location may be unknown.

As there are no very old people living around the church who were born in the neighborhood, local tradition could not be drawn in. Perhaps Mrs. Harry Nein, in the county home, holds the key to the mystery. If Dolly Snyder's grave is found, then Regina's will be known and properly honored. She deserves a monument, yea, a simple marker, just as much as Mary Jemison, "the White Woman of the Genessee," a girl who was captured by Indians, successively married two of them, Sheninjee and Hiokatoo, and lived the life of a squaw, does that imposing pile of marble and bronze in Letchworth Park, in New York State. Once, a simple country school master planned to put up a slab in memory of the "Blue Mountain Captive" in the cemetery wall, but he went away, and the project was forgotten.

Before resuming our way through Stouchsburg to Bernville, the "Nordkill" of history, we were driven to the site of the home of Kate Edwards,[118] who killed her husband and languished in Reading Jail for thirteen years, only being liberated this year. The house is gone, the well where the victim's body was thrown is almost filled up, and a field of swaying rye hides and smiles over it all. Only the stone quarry where

118. On September 19, 1901, it took the jury two hours of deliberation to reach the verdict of guilty for Kate Edwards of the first-degree murder on July 3, 1901, of her husband John Edwards, and they imposed the death penalty for the brutal slaying. Standing before the jury, it was reported that she received the verdict with the greatest coolness and stolid demeanor. The principal witnesses against her were two of her children, 15-year-old Mary and 12-year-old Elmer, whose testimony convicted her. John Edwards was intoxicated that night and fell asleep on the front porch of their home, after which Kate wrapped his head in a carpet and beat him to death with a hammer. She then buried the bloody carpet, hammer and the dress she had worn to do the deed. Kate Edwards was never executed for her crime. She became very religious while in jail and was reported to have been a model prisoner. She was pardoned on October 25, 1913, and released from jail. (The Boyertown Area Expression)

the colored paramour worked remains.[119] The world is "wax to receive, marble to retain," as Lord Byron used to say.

On the way to Bernville, we passed a newly-cut hay field, which was dotted with killdeer and flickers. The killdeers flew up at our approach, "peeping" mournfully. These night-crying birds are said to contain the souls of dead Indians and are locally known as Killorees.

119. At Kate's trial, the prosecution called Samuel Greason as a witness. Greason admitted that he would often visit the Edwards home on Saturday evenings to drink with them, and that he and Kate had been intimate on those evenings after John Edwards had passed out. He also testified that Kate had written a letter to him suggesting that he come visit soon, at which time they could "get the old man drunk and then throw him into the cistern." He stated that Kate frequently complained to him about her husband and had said they had not lived as husband and wife for over a year. Kate Edwards was convicted of first-degree murder and sentenced to death. Before her trial, Kate Edwards gave birth in prison to a dark-skinned baby girl, whom she named Alma. For many years to come, Alma would live in jail with her mother. Following Kate Edwards' conviction, Greason was tried on the theory that he had been her accomplice in the murder of her husband. At Greason's trial, Kate Edwards testified that Greason had been the one to actually kill her husband, and that the two of them had then taken his body to the cistern together. On December 20, 1901, Greason was convicted of murder and sentenced to death. On appeal, Greason's conviction was affirmed. Ten times, Greason had the date set for his execution, only to have it delayed each time. In February 1905, on the day before Greason was to be executed, Kate Edwards formally recanted the testimony in which she claimed Greason had killed her husband. She admitted Greason had not been involved and that she alone had committed the murder. Based on this recantation, Greason was granted a new trial and, on June 16, 1905, was acquitted.

REHRERSBURG

UNION CANAL AT STOUCHSBURG

Arrived Bernville

Red Kay Hotel good. A grand, old-style town.

7:00 P.M.

WE stopped at the sign of the "red K" at old Bernville, formerly the Eagle Hotel.[120] Now it is kept by Harry Redcay,[121] a former acrobat, hence the name. Mr. Redcay is a kindly man and made us feel at home.

In the evening, we strolled along the quiet street, meeting Mr. F. H. Wagner,[122] the local Justice of the Peace and a noted veteran of the Civil War, with whom we conversed pleasantly for some time.

---

120. The hotel is now known as the Bernville Eagle Hotel.

121. Harry Blaine Redcay (November 29, 1884 – March 1951) is buried in Oley Cemetery in Spangsville.

122. Frank H. Wagner (February 12, 1838 – June 19, 1926) is buried at Friedens Union Church in Shartlesville.

EAGLE HOTEL IN BERNVILLE

Left Bernville

Interesting road to Reading via Scull's Hill and Half-Way House. Excellent roads.

June 22, 8:30 A.M.

THE rain was falling softly when we departed the following morning, but we could see how the country looked under such conditions. We drove along the slope of Scull's Hill, mentioned by Bayard Taylor, which forms the central eminence of the Berks landscape, stopped for a moment at the quaint old Bern Church, where above the graveyard gate are these words: "Remember That We All Are Mortal." At the Half-Way House, built in 1843, we turned to the right in the direction of Reading, which was seven miles away, our week in the Blue Mountains almost a thing of the past.

All the way into town, we met many birds flying about "after the rain," for the clouds were now lifting. We had kept a record of the number we had seen, also wild animals, and it totaled as follows: Buzzards, 26; Red-Headed Woodpeckers, 28; Flickers, 27: Green Herons, 3; Ruffed Grouse, 2; Quails, 29; Blue Birds, 5; Red-Winged Blackbirds, 10; Mourning Doves, 8; Night Hawks, 5; Goldfinches, 9; Baltimore Orioles, 14; Cowbird, 1; Spotted Sandpipers, 6; Killdeers, 15; Brown 7'hriislies, 18; Upland Plovers, 10; Red-Shouldered Hawks, 2; Sparrow Hawks, 3; Rabbits, 9; Red Squirrels, 20; Gray Squirrels, 5; Water Snake, 1; Turtles, 5.

These, all told, would barely make a "bag" for the modern, rapacious pothunter. We made no record of the commoner species of birds, like robins, meadow larks, blackbirds, sparrows and so on, or of chipmunks.

Arrived Reading

Stopped at American House.

10:45 A.M.

BUT now the smokes and stacks of Reading rise before us, and we hear the distant roar of the town. We pass the Country Club, the new Bright residence, the Driscoll estate, the Magdalen Home in rapid succession[123] and, almost before we know it, are crossing the Schuylkill Avenue Bridge.

Through a maze of paved streets, amid motors, trucks, buggies and noises, we thread our way; once more, we are in front of the American House. Friendly faces greet us there, to hear all about our trip; it is all over but the memories, which are indestructible. And many a day, or year, if we live, will that week in the wistful, splendid Blue Mountains rise before us, setting a standard of peaceful, sane enjoyment that brought us well-nigh to the portal of true happiness, the abode of the angels. We have been raised to a higher spiritual plane, which, please God, we may always keep. Let us hold our ambitions and dreams on a level with the highest point of the grand old mountains, which we love, where our ancestors lived and died, and we will find content in this earthly sphere.

123. Today, this is Route 183 (the Bernville Road) that becomes Schuylkill Avenue after crossing the river.

THE AMERICAN HOUSE HOTEL AT 4TH AND PENN

Index

www.ingramcontent.com/pod-product-compliance
Lightning Source LLC
LaVergne TN
LVHW052348100826
845147LV00012B/781

9798888194485